Naughty Adult Joke Book #9:

Dirty, Funny, and Slutty Jokes That Made You Play Golf with Your Boss

Check out other adult joke books:

<u>Naughty Adult Joke Book: Dirty, Slutty, Funny Jokes That
Broke The Censors</u> – Jason S. Jones

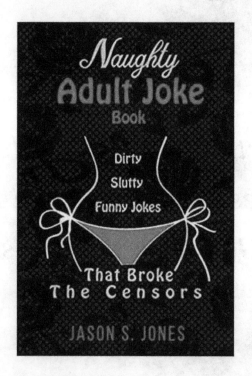

Why is a vagina similar to bad weather?

Once it wets, you have to go in.

3

Introduction

Congratulations on purchasing the *Naughty Adult Joke Book #9: Dirty, Funny, And Slutty Jokes That Made You Play Golf with Your Boss*, and thank you for doing so. The workplace has so many inside jokes, but the rest of the world assumes that people are always serious, because they do not get the jokes, and even if they did, it is difficult to understand many of them because they have some hard work-related terms. However, this book compiles some of the best easiest-to-understand work and office jokes that will have you and your boss rolling on the floor in laughter.

You will see that the majority of these jokes provide context, unlike those in other books in this series. The thing is that, for you to get what is happening, we must paint a picture of what is happening, or what is the norm, so that you can see the satire, the irony, or the plain funny in each of these jokes. As advertised, the jokes herein are very dirty and slutty, to tickle your naughty mind, but others are just some good-natured, yet hilarious jokes.

The following chapters present a comprehensive list of the funniest workplace-themed jokes from different professions. It will not only make you understand the environment in each of these professions; you will also get to learn and understand what happens in each of the workplaces described below.

Now, get ready to laugh your way through the book, and remember to share these jokes with your spouse, friends, and family. Spread the cheer!

There are plenty of books on this subject on the market, so thanks again for choosing this one! Every effort was made to ensure it is full of as much useful information as possible. Please, enjoy!

Chapter 1:One-Liners, Puns, and Other Jokes

Section 1: One-Liners

Q: What should a lawyer do that a duck can't, but a goose can?
A: Shove the bill up the ass!

Q: Which letter of the alphabet do pirates love the most?
A: You might assume that it is the letter 'R,' but they prefer the 'C.'

Q: What lured the woman into going out for a date with a mushroom?
A: She found him to be a fun-ghi.

Q: Which mode of transportation does the potato prefer?
A: The gravy train.

Q: What did the empty glass say to the full glass?
A: Dude, you're drunk.

Q: What did you hear about a constipated accountant?
A: When he was unable to budget, he opted to work it out with a pencil and a paper.

Q: What did the ocean say to the other ocean?
A: Nothing, the oceans only waved.

Q: What is the difference between a stripper and a waitress working at the strip club?
A: Just two weeks.

Q: What name is given to an IT teacher who insists on touching his students inappropriately?
A: A PDF file!

Q: What does a puppy and a near-sighted gynecologist have in common?
A: A wet nose.

Q: Why is it dangerous to fall for a tennis player?
A: Because to a tennis player... Love means NOTHING!

Q: Why is it so difficult for pirates to study the alphabet?

A: They tend to spend all their time at 'C.'

Q: Why was the toilet paper unable to cross the road?
A: It had been stuck on a crack.

Q: Why could the bike not go anywhere?
A: The bike was two-tired.

Q: What was the reason did the calendar factory give for firing that guy?
A: He had taken a day off.

Q: What is the common factor between politicians and diapers?
A: Both stink and require changing more often.

Q: If an accountant's wife is having trouble sleeping, which is the most effective and quickest remedy to help her sleep sooner?
A: Ask her husband to talk about his work.

Q: What made the lawyer carefully skim the Bible just before he died?
A: He was looking to see if there were any loopholes.

Q: How is a genealogist different from a gynecologist?
A: The genealogist examines the family tree, while the gynecologist examines the family bush.

Q: What name do you give to a lawyer who does not know the law?
A: The Judge.

Q: What made the can crusher walk out on his job?
A: He said it was soda pressing.

Q: What made the boy wrap himself up in wrapping paper on his birthday?
A: His friends had asked him to live in the present.

Q: Why are lawyers not attacked by sharks?
A: The sharks are exercising professional courtesy.

Q: Why does Chuck Norris have problems using the Internet?
A: He refuses to submit.

Q: Why are you likely to starve when you are in the desert?

A: There is so much sand there.

Q: What have you when about 100 lawyers are buried in the sand up to their necks?
A: Insufficient sand.

Q: What makes chemists such good problem solvers?
A: The chemists have all the solutions!

Q: What do you do to earn yourself a small fortune when trading in the stock market?
A: Have a big fortune to begin with.

Q: What did one eye say to the other?
A: Between you and me, I can honestly say that something smells.

Q: Usually, what does the house put on?
A: A dress.

Q: How is your job just like Christmas?
A: You have to do all the hard work, but the fat guy in a suit takes all the credit.

Q: What made the scarecrow get the promotion?
A: He was most outstanding in the field.

Q: Did you hear about the man that broke in and stole a calendar?
A: Yeah, he only got 12 months!

Q: Why are there only two doors on a Chicken Coop?
A: Because if two more doors were added, making four, it would be called a "Chicken Sedan"!

Q: What do construction workers do when they party?
A: Raise the roof.

Q: Would a Kangaroo be able to jump higher than a house?
A: Sure! The house would not be able to jump at all.

Q: Had Bert Newton been a butcher, how would he have introduced his wife in social gatherings?
A: Here, meat Patty!

Q: What made the developer go broke?
A: He had used up all the cache.

Q: What is the name given to a bear that got no teeth?

A: A gummy bear!

Section 2: Puns and Short Jokes

I had been lying on my bed all night trying to figure out at what point of the universe the sun was. I was surprised when it dawned on me.

I enjoy pressing F5; it is quite refreshing.

I now appreciate the fact that worrying works! 90% of the things I spend time distressing about do not happen.

I went to see the doctor and told him that my arm had broken in two places. His advice was that I should cease going to those places.

Being an astronaut is one of the strangest jobs in the world. They fire you even before you begin working.

Before you sit down to criticize someone, it would be nice if you tried to walk a mile in the person's shoes. That way, when you start to criticize them, you will have their shoes and will be a mile away.

My resume is simply a list of things that I sure hope no one ever asks me to do.

I do not work well under pressure... Or any other condition.

Artificial intelligence does not stand a chance against natural stupidity.

Two antennas chose to get married to each other. Their wedding ceremony was so boring, but the reception thereafter was great!

Whenever you are in doubt, just mumble.

Keep your dreams alive by hitting the snooze button.

I did not say that it is your fault. I only said that I blame you.

You will never be too old to learn some completely stupid things.

If someone is smiling in a crisis, he has found somebody to blame.

Some mistakes are just too fun for you to make just once.

Working for an entire week is often so rough that, after doing Monday and Tuesday, the calendar itself is so exhausted it says, WTF!

A man is excited to take his family out to the zoo. However, on getting there, they find that the entire zoo has only one exhibit. They realized that this was a Shih Tzu.

A corporation is just like a tree that is full of monkeys, each on a different level. The monkeys sitting at the top of the tree look down and all they see is a tree full of happy smiling monkeys. The monkeys sitting on the bottom levels look up, and all they see are assholes.

If you are able to remain calm when everything else around you is in chaos, you probably haven't understood what is going on.

To ensure that you have hit the target, shoot whatever is in your way, and call it the target.

A doctor slides his hand down his smock to get a pen so that he can use it to write a prescription. To his dismay, he pulls out a rectal thermometer. "Holy shit!" he exclaims, "Some asshole's got my pen!"

Laugh when you got problems — everyone else does, too.

No one ever died from working hard, but why would you risk it?

Experience is the thing you get when you fail to get what you hoped to get.

If it was not for the last minute, nothing could be done around here?

A guy rings his boss at work.
Employee: Sorry Boss, but I am unable to report to work today. I am seriously sick.
Boss: Oh, really? What's happening with you this time?
Employee: I got anal glaucoma.
Boss: Mmmh... And what is that?
Employee: I really don't see my ass working at the moment.

I did not work today because I had an eye problem. The issue was that I couldn't see myself working today.

A man has the capacity to do even more than he thinks he can, but typically, he does much less than he assumes he does.

A thief walked up to a man and stuck his gun to the man's ribs. He yelled at him, "Hand me all your money!" The man was shaken by this sudden attack, and he said, "Please don't do this, I am a congressman!"
"In that case," the thief replied, "Hand me my money!"

I crawled out of my bed and got dressed. What more do you want from me?

Progress is what lazy people make when they are seeking a shortcut for doing things.

Once in a while, everything that could possibly go wrong does, along with two or three other things that couldn't possibly.

I am so sorry I missed your call. I had gone to visit my doctor to have my heart and brain taken out so that I can stand a chance to get the recently-vacated management position.

Sometimes, the best form of helping hand you can lend is a firm shove.

If you really want to play a dirty trick on your coworkers, stick a 'Please Use the Other Door' sign at the office building entrance, especially if the building only has one entrance.

A guy is at the hospital visiting a friend, and while there, he takes notice of some very pretty nurses. He also noticed that each of them wore a pin that was designed in the shape of an apple. He asks one of the nurses, "What does your pin signify?" The nurse answers, "Oh! It's nothing," she chuckles and continues, "We only use it to keep the doctors away."

I always thought that my goal was to build a career. I didn't realize that all I wanted were paychecks.

The problem with punctuality is that you won't get anyone there to appreciate you.

I am standing outside an office waiting for a job interview. Once I am done, and I do not get the job, kindly be prepared to handle my mood.

An archeologist is a professional whose career lies in ruins.

Whenever the boss makes any mistake, we all made it.

When you cannot convince them, confuse them.

Employee: Hey, Sir, may I please take a day off in the coming week, to visit my mother-in-law?
Boss: No, you cannot!
Employee: Oh, thank you so much, Boss. I was certain that you would understand.

Although maintaining a positive attitude does not solve any problems, it does annoy enough people, and this makes it worth the effort.

If your feet are firmly pressed on the ground, it will be difficult for you to put on your pants.

The definition of a committee is the gathering of twelve people to do one person's work.

An office had just hired a new office-boy, and one afternoon, he came into the boss's office and announced, "Sir, I think someone wants to talk to you on the phone."

The boss shook his head and demanded, "What do you mean by 'you think'?"

"You see, Sir," the boy answered, "When I picked the phone, the voice at the other end asked, 'Am I talking to you, you old fool?'"

I love work because it fascinates me. I could sit and gaze at it for many hours.

It matters not whether you win or lose; the only thing that matters is whether I do.

If you don't succeed the first time, redefine success.

I got no solution, but I sure do admire the problem.

My boss is not usually happy with anyone that yells, "Hey weirdo!" because too many people look up and are distracted from their work.

If you are feeling stressed out, the solution is to make a cup of nice steaming tea and then spilling it on the lap of the person bugging you.

When you get to work, always remember that change is inevitable, except when you use the vending machine.

It is never about how god you work; it is all about how well you explain what you have done.

Bosses have the tendency to make rules for their juniors, and exemptions for themselves.

A diplomat is a person that can tell you to go to hell in such a good way that you actually look forward to it.

When I started out, I had nothing, and I still got a lot of it.

To human is to err, but to blame it on another person is a sign of management potential.

One day at my workplace, our computers were down, and we had to do everything manually. I took 20 minutes to shuffle the cards so we could play Solitaire.

Drink lots of coffee. It allows you to do the silly things faster, and with more vigor!

Some people get to learn from the mistakes of others. The rest of us are the others.
We already got enough youth. How about we now get a fountain of 'smart?'

It may not seem like it, but I do indeed get plenty of exercise. I am busy dodging deadlines, pushing my luck, and jumping to conclusions.

Efficiency is the advanced form of laziness.

If each day we are alive is a gift, I want to have the receipt for Monday so that I can exchange it and get another Friday.

When you are prompted and want to fight fire with fire, be wise, and remember that the fire department uses water.

Whenever I hire someone into my company, I always tell them, don't think of me as the boss, think of me as your friend who can fire you.

The best way to use your stress ball is to throw it on the head of the individual that upset you last.

Little Johnny approached his mom and asked, "Momma, must all fairy tales start with 'once upon a time?"
The mom replied, "Of course not, dear. Some start with 'Sweetheart, I will be at the office working late tonight...'"

I have perfected my multitasking ability. I can be unproductive, procrastinate, and waste time all at the same time.

While some say that the glass is half-full and others say it is half-empty, engineers say that the glass is actually twice as big as it needs to be.

Nothing takes down the Friday mood than the realization that today is only Monday.

Discretion is the ability to raise only an eyebrow when you want to raise your voice.

Johnny calls the doctor's office to make his appointment. The receptionist receives the call on the other end and says, "I am so sorry, Sir... we are not in a position to fit you into our schedule — at least not for the next two weeks." Johnny protests, "But I could be dead by that time!" "Don't worry about that, Sir. You could ask your wife to call us so that we can cancel the appointment."

My son told me that, when he grows up, he wants to become a secret agent. Based on that statement alone, I doubt he would make a good secret agent.

The reason I 'nod off to sleep' when I am in a boring meeting is to make it look like I agree to every boring detail being said.

My boss was lecturing me one day, and he said to me that there is no such thing as problems; they are all opportunities. I told him, "Mmh... That's cool. Well, I guess I got a serious drinking opportunity."

Whenever I am filing an employment application, and I am asked to indicate who is to be notified in case of an emergency, I write, "A very good doctor."

All I need is a chance to prove to you all that money cannot make me happy.

When my boss fired me from my job at the unemployment office last Friday, he said to me, "Empty out your desk, and I will see you on Monday."

I quit the job I had at the helium gas factory. I could not stand being talked to in that tone of voice!

My boss rudely remarked that I am preoccupied with a vengeance. Well, we'll see about that.

I enjoy my time at work. Lately, my colleagues have begun writing names on the foods they place in the office fridge. Today, I am eating a yogurt whose name is Susan. How cool is that?

I approached my company's corporate wellness officer and asked, "Could you please teach me yoga?" He asked, "How flexible are you?" I answered, "I cannot make Thursdays."

The person who has stolen my Microsoft Office must pay for it... And you have my Word.

My memory has deteriorated to the point that I have lost my job. I still am employed, I just don't remember where.

Retirement sounds so good. You do nothing all day without fear of getting caught.

I have no problems going to work every day; it is the 8-hour wait to get home that I cannot stand.

When I got into this job and had to use a paperless office, all was going great until when it was time to use the bathroom.

I saw my annual performance appraisal, and it says that I lack intensity and passion. It must be because the management is yet to see me with a Big Mac when I am alone.

One day, while at the office, my colleague got a call, and on the other side was a woman who sounded every bit confused. She asked, "Who are you?"

"My name is John. With whom would you like to speak?"

There was a long pause before the woman spoke again. She asked, "Did you just say 'whom'?"

Confused, my coworker answered, "Ye...es! I did."

"Well, I must have the wrong number." She hung up.

An office placed its vacancy advertisement and was receiving many applications. A guy went there also, and the manager interviewing him asked, "Would you tell me what Ph.D. means?"

The guy answered, "It means Passed High School with Difficulties."

My boss and I were arguing one day when he asked me who was the stupid one between him and I. I laughed, and reassured him that the company's employees all understand that the boss does not hire any stupid persons.

I got into my workplace early today morning, and my boss came storming through the door to my office and asked,

"Yesterday, you missed work, didn't you?" I answered, "No, not really."

Yesterday, at my job, I caught a coworker being horribly inefficient. I said to him, "Dude, what you are doing is undeniably slowing you down." The guy replied, "Yes, I know. I am working on the kitchen remodeling, and I ought to be counterproductive."

If you are at a job interview, assure the panel that you will give 110 percent of your dedication... Unless you have applied to the statistician position.

The issue with doing things right the first time is that no one appreciates how hard it was.

Boss: People claim that there is life after death. Do you believe that?
Me: Not really. There is no proof of that.
Boss: Well, you gotta believe it because you took the day off the other day to go to your grandmother's funeral and — she is now on the phone looking for you.

I like to pretend that I am working for as long as they pretend to be paying me.

A new employee is interacting with her colleagues, with each party trying to know the other well. The topic of her former workplace comes up, when one of the workers asks her why she left her previous job. "I left because my boss said something," the woman replied.
"Oh, really? What did that boss say about you?"
"You are fired!"

The human brain is a remarkable organ. It works perfectly from the time you are born without stopping, up until when you stand to speak in public.

Walking down the street, a man saw the sign 'Help Wanted' stuck on a store window. The man ran into the store and yelled, "What's wrong?"

I bet I was picked for my superior motivational skills. The people around me say that whenever I am around, they got to work two times harder.

One of the hardest things to do when it comes to doing business is to mind yours.

If you have a calendar, your days are numbered.

When my road worker's father was accused of stealing from his job, I could not believe these allegations. However, when I got home, the signs were all there.

"What would you like to become when you grow up?"
"A medical doctor."
"Why would you want to become a doctor?"
"Because that is the only profession in which you are allowed to ask women to remove their clothes and proceed to stick the bill with their husbands."

Many people stop looking for work the minute they land a job.

In employment, my biggest ambition is to have a desk that does not allow anyone to see my computer monitor except for me.

I got so many jokes about the unemployed, but not even one works.

The end-of-year party at work is always fun because it gives you an opportunity to see and interact with people you have barely seen in the last 20 minutes.

Avoid walking in front of me because I might not follow. Avoid walking behind me because I might not lead. Avoid walking beside me. Pretty much leave me alone and let me be.

I will not have the opportunity to delete all the emails you will have sent me until when I am back from my vacation. Kindly be patient, and I will delete the mail in the order you sent it.

New Employer: In this post, we are looking to have a responsible person.
Job Applicant: I am happy to say that your search ends today. The job I held previously, whenever something went wrong, all my colleagues would say that I was responsible.

Just when you are certain that you are able to make ends meet, some ignorant fool comes and shifts the ends.
To an adequately endowed fool: Nothing is foolproof.

An employee walks up to his supervisor and says, "Boss, my wife and I are doing some deep house-cleaning tomorrow, and she needs me there to help with the garage, the attic, and to haul and move stuff." The supervisor responds, "Sorry, but you cannot take the day off. We are short-handed." The employee responds, "Thank you, Sir. I knew I could count on you."

The farther the future is from here, the better it appears.

If everything appears to be coming your way, it must be because you are on the wrong lane.

It's not about who you know, it is about whom you know.

A philosopher and a scientist are in the wild, and a lion is in hot pursuit of them. The scientist begins to make some quick mental calculations and says, "It is not worth trying to outrun it. The animal is catching up!" The philosopher is now running a little bit ahead, and he says, "I don't care about outrunning the lion — I just have to outrun you!"

A guy is in for his job interview, sitting across his would-be boss.
The boss asks, "Which would you say is your worst quality?"
The guy answers, "I can be too honest."
The boss answers, "I don't think that is a bad quality; honesty is one of the good qualities."
The guy replies, "Well, I really don't give a crap about what you think of me!"

I was invited to a job interview last week, and when we began to discuss salary, the interviewer said that I would be getting a salary of $2,000 per month, and that after 6 months, the company would raise my salary to $2,500. I told him that I would start the job in six months.

Section 3: Long Jokes

Pick 'Em Up

A boss approached his secretary with a proposition. He said, "Let me have sex with you. It will be very fast. I will just throw some 1,000 dollars on the floor, and you pick it up. By the time you are done, I will be done, also."

The girl requested she be given some time to think about it. When the boss left, the secretary called her boyfriend and informed him about the boss' proposal. The boyfriend thought this to be harmless, but on condition that she asks him for 2,000 dollars instead. She would pick the money so fast that by the time she was done, the man would not even have undressed her. When the plan was sealed, the girl walked into her boss' office for the planned exchange.

An hour passes, and the anxious boyfriend calls his girlfriend and asks, "Why haven't you called back? What happened?" The girlfriend responds, "I am still picking the money up. The bastard used coins, and he still is having sex with me!"

The Boss Parrot

A man walks into a pet shop to get himself a parrot. He finds in the shop three identical parrots on a perch, but they all got different prices. The storeowner points to one and says, "This parrot costs $500."

The man is surprised by this quotation, and he asks, "Why is that parrot so expensive?"

The storeowner answers, "He can use a computer."

The man is impressed, but proceeds to ask about the second parrot. The store owner informs him that the second parrot costs 1,000 dollars because it does everything that the first parrot does, and in addition, it can use the UNIX operating system.

The already-startled man continued on to ask about the third parrot. He was told its price was $2,000.

Naturally, the man asked what this parrot could do. The owner replied, "I have to be honest with you. I really have not seen it do anything special, but these two call him 'Boss'!"

I Bet

Employee: "Boss, I bet you $6,000 that I could piss in a cup placed thirty meters away."

Boss: "Alright, I'd love to see you do it."

(The employee moves around the floor pissing, and this automatically causes him to lose the $6,000. However, the employee doesn't seem to care about what happens.)

Boss: "Ha! Not even a drop got to the cup. You lost the $6,000."

Secretary: "Oh SHIT!"

Boss: "What's up?"

Secretary: "We had bet $200,000 that he could piss all over your floor, and you would be smiling about it!"

Screw Me, I Screw You

A guy finds his way to a restaurant bar and leans over the counter. He asks the bartender, "How much do you charge for a beer?"

The bartender tells him that it costs a dollar.

The guy is amazed by the low price, and he orders one. He then asks the bartender, "Well, how much do you charge for the New York sirloin served with some salad and mashed potatoes, together with a slice of cheesecake for dessert?"

The bartender says to him, "Just five dollars."

Again, the guy is completely shocked by the prices. His meal is brought forward, and when he is done eating his meal, he says, "Wow! I really love this place. It is so amazing! Unimaginable prices and everything taste so good. Would you help me meet the business owner?"

The bartender answers him, "Oh, the guy is in his office upstairs with my wife."

The guy is now confused and he asks, "Why is he upstairs with your wife?"

The bartender replies, "Well, he is doing the same thing I am doing to his business."

Three Companies after Me

Bill makes his way into his boss's office and says to him, "Sir, I gotta be straight with you. I am aware that the economy is not doing too well, but three companies are after me. I respectfully want to ask for a raise. The due haggles for a few minutes, and the boss finally agree to give Bill a 5 percent raise on his pay. Bill is very happy with that offer. He gets up to leave, and when he is almost at the door, his boss asks, "If I may ask, which are those three companies that are after you?"
Bill grins and says, "The water company, the electricity company, and the phone company."

Idiots Fall Away

At the Army Base, a group of soldiers is standing in formation. The Drill Sergeant comes up and shouts, "All idiots, fall out!" The soldiers all wander away, but for one soldier who maintains his place and remains attention. The Drill Sergeant walks up to him and comes so close until the duo is eye to eye. The sergeant raises a single eyebrow. Seeing this, the soldier smiles and says, "There sure was a lot of 'em, Sir, huh?"

Quick Loan

A businessman was planning his trip to Europe. He was
going there on business. He drove to a New York City Bank
in his Rolls Royce and went in to request an immediate
5000-dollar loan. His loans officer was taken aback by the
immediate request, and he asked for collateral.

The man handed him the keys to his Rolls Royce for
collateral. The loan officer accepted the collateral, and asked
that the car be driven into the bank's secret underground
parking, and he handed the businessman some five thousand
dollars.

Two weeks pass, and the man is back, walking down the
banking halls. He asked if he could settle his loan so he could
get his Rolls Royce back.

The loan officer said to him, "Since you have repaid your
loan promptly, you will be charged $15.40 in addition to the
principal amount of $5,000."

The businessman took out his checkbook and wrote a check
for the total amount. He thanked the loan officer and stood
to walk away. Before he could open the door, the loan officer
called out to him and said, "Sir, would you kindly wait for a
moment?" The man stood in his tracks and turned to the
loan officer to hear what he was saying.

"I did a research on you and found out that you were a millionaire. Why did you have to borrow the five thousand dollars, Sir?"

The rich man smiled at him and replied, "There is nowhere else in Manhattan that I could safely park my Rolls Royce for the two weeks I was away for $15.40."

Preferred Patients

Three doctors are hanging out in the break room talking about their favorite types of patients. The first doctor says, "I personally like attending to librarians; their organs are all alphabetized."

The second doctor says, "I like to attend to mathematicians; their organs are all numbered."

The third doctor speaks up and says, "I love to treat lawyers; they are brainless, gutless, spineless, heartless, and you could interchange their rear-ends with their heads."

The New Location

An entrepreneur was opening his small business, and one of his friends made an order to have flowers delivered to the business to wish his friend luck and to mark this wonderful occasion.

The flowers were delivered at the location of the new business, and the owner received them with delight. However, he was surprised to see that the accompanying card read, "Rest in Peace." The business owner was horrified, and he rang his friend to tell him what the card read. As expected, the friend was raging mad, too, and he rang the florist to complain.

After he had explained his case, and expressed his frustrations, the florist said, "Sir, I apologize for that grave mistake, but instead of getting angry, think about it like this: There is a funeral taking place in another location, and the flowers sent there have a note that reads, "Congratulations on your new location!"

The Interviews

A businessman is conducting interviews for all the applicants who have applied to the managerial post in one of his company's larger divisions. The businessman came up with a foolproof test that would allow him to quickly determine which of the candidates was best suited for this position. To each applicant, he would simply ask, "What is two plus two?"

The first applicant who came up was a journalist. He gave his answer, "Twenty-two."

The second interviewee worked as a social worker. She answered, "I may not know the answer to that question, but I am sure glad that we have the opportunity to talk about it."

The third interviewee who walked in was an engineer. When he heard the question, he reached for his bag and took out a slide ruler. Five minutes in, he turned to the interviewer and said, "It's got to be something between 3.9999 and 4.0001."

The fourth interviewee that walked in was an attorney. He said, "In the *Jenkins vs. The Department of the Treasury*, it was proven that two plus two is four."

The fifth and final interviewee was an accountant. When the question was posed to him, he stood up from his chair and headed for the door. He shut it, walked back to his seat, sat

down, and leaning across the table, he whispered to the interviewer, "How much would you want it to be?
The accountant got the job.

Practice While Waiting

A lawyer is in the box office, standing in a very long queue. He suddenly feels a pair of hands kneading his neck, shoulders, and down to his back. He turns around and asks, "What the heck are you doing?"
"I don't mean to upset you, Sir, I am a chiropractor, and I love to keep in practice as I wait in line."
The now angry lawyer replies, "So? I am a lawyer, but I am not trying to screw the guy standing in front of me!"

The Complimentary Nuts

A guy enters a bar, and since it is still quite early, the bar is literary empty, but for him and the bartender arranging the drinks at the counter. The man sits down on a stool and orders a drink.
As he is waiting for his drink, he hears a whisper, "Pssst... Your tie is so pretty." The man looks around to see if someone is there, but there is no one behind him.

A moment passes, and again, he hears, "Pssst... That color on your shirt looks really nice on you."

The guy turns to the bartender and asks him, "Hey, dude... Have you spoken to me?"

The bartender looks at him, rolls his eyes, and gives a sigh.

He says, "I'm so sorry, Sir. It's the peanuts... They are complementary."

The Light Bulb

Two workers in a factory are having a conversation. The lady says, "I bet I can make the boss give me the rest of the day off." The man jeers at her and asks, "And how would you go about that?"

"You just wait and see."

The lady hangs upside down with her legs on the ceiling. When the boss comes in, he asks, "Why are you doing that?"

"I am a light bulb," the lady replies.

The boss is astounded by this. He says, "You have worked so hard you've gone crazy. You need to take the rest of the day off."

The man comes down and follows the lady on the way home. The boss asks him where he is going. The man replies, "I got to head home, too; I cannot work in the dark."

Send a Bill

A lawyer and a doctor are chatting at a party when a group of people come up and disrupt their conversation. The people start to describe their ailments, and they begin to seek free medical advice from the doctor. An hour into this, the doctor is already frustrated. The doctor leans towards the lawyer and asks, "How do you keep people from asking for legal advice outside of your office?"

The lawyer replies, "Whenever I give them advice, I send a bill." The doctor is surprised by this answer, but he decides to try it, anyway. The next day, despite feeling a little guilty, the doctor starts to prepare the bills. On opening the mailbox to place the bills, the man finds a bill the lawyer sent.

The Screw

A woman enters her doctor's office and starts talking to him about the facelift she wants. The doctor is optimistic about the procedure, and he says, "Well, I could do your facelift, but you would need to come back for a follow-up in about six months."

The woman doesn't like the idea of a follow-up, and she says, "Oh no! I would like it done in a single shot. I do not wish to repeat the procedure again."

The doctor is taken by this response, but he offers a solution. He says, "Turns out there is a new procedure in which I could drill a screw through the top of your head, and anytime you see some wrinkles appearing on your face, you will only need to turn the screw. Doing this will pull your skin a little bit tighter, and the wrinkles will be gone.

"Oh! That sounds easier! I would want that! Let's do it, doctor!"

Six months pass, and the lady marches into the doctor's office.

On seeing her, the doctor rises from his seat to greet her. He excitedly asks her, "How is your procedure serving you?"

The lady is upset, and she bellows, "It's terrible! Got to be the worst mistake I ever made."

Why? What's up?" the doctor enquires.

The lady points to her face and says, "Just look at the bags I have beneath my eyes!"

The doctor retorts back, "Lady, those are your boobs, not bags. If you do not stop turning that screw, you will soon have a beard."

Stop or Slow Down?

A lawyer was on the road, and he runs a stop sign. The sheriff of the area pulls him over. As you would expect, the big shot New York attorney thinks that he has had better education and is, therefore, smarter, and better placed than the West Virginia sheriff. The sheriff asked the driver to hand him his license and registration. The lawyer finds this ludicrous and asks, "What for?"

The sheriff replies, "Because you failed to come to a complete stop upon reaching the stop sign."

"I slowed down," the lawyer defends himself, "But there was no one coming."

"Still, you failed to come to a complete stop," the sheriff insists. "Get me your license and registration, please."

The lawyer is indignant, and says, "I will give you the license and registration if you can prove to the difference between stop and slowing down. After that, if you deem it necessary, you could still give me a ticket. If not, I get to go."

The sheriff agrees to the deal and says, "Well, that is a fair deal. Now, please exit your vehicle, Sir."

The lawyer gets out of his car, and the sheriff grabs a hold of his nightstick. He starts beating the lawyer with the stick all over his body. The sheriff asks, "Now, would you like me to stop or just to slow down?"

Advanced Technology

A guy is sitting next to his wife in the lounge, talking about the events of the day. Suddenly, the wife rouses from where she is seated and says to the man, "Please, got get me a newspaper."

The tech-savvy husband is perturbed by that request. He asks, "Just how backward are you! Technology is so advanced, yet you ask me to fetch you a newspaper... Use my iPad instead."

The wife picks the iPad and slams it on the floor to kill a cockroach. The husband passes out.

Las Vegas

A man had gone to Las Vegas on a business trip. Prior to this trip, the man had been enquiring about Las Vegas, and one of the things that had stood out was about how awesome the whores in Las Vegas were. Therefore, that very first day he arrived, when evening came, he decided to go out and try his luck. The man walked out of the hotel, and as he looked out into the street, there stood an attractive girl at the street corner.

The man approached the girl and asked if she was on business, and sure enough, the girl was working. She asked him to meet her in room 804 in the hotel across the street. The man thought he was in luck because the girl was a knockout. When the duo got to the room, the man anxiously sat at the edge of the bed. The girl came up and asked the man to state what he wanted. The man was quiet for a moment before he spoke up and said, "How many dollars for a handjob?"

"300," she said.

The man was so shocked his eyes popped open. He asked, "300?"

The girl answered, "Stand up, walk to the window and open those curtains." The man did as was asked.

The girl said, "Do you see the motel there? It is mine, and it was not passed down to me... I'm good."

The man was impressed, and he said to her, "Alright, go right ahead, sweetheart." The lady bent down and gave the man the handjob of a lifetime. It was better than he had imagined.

The duo rested a while, and the man started thinking aloud in his mind. He wondered how good a blowjob would be if a handjob was that good. He turned to the girl and asked, "What do you charge for a blowjob?"

The girl stroked his chest hairs and answered, "600 bucks!"

"Oh, Lord!" the man exclaimed.

The lady asked the man to walk over to the window. She asked, "Do you see that 15-storey hotel there? It is mine, and it was not passed down to me. I am that good."

The man was impressed. He said, "Alright, sweetie, let's get to work."

Just as he expected, the blowjob was phenomenal. It was the best he had ever had.

The couple lay on the bed for a second resting time, and the man's mind starts running wild again. He started to think just how awesome sex would be if the blowjob and the handjob had been that amazing. He asked, "How much do you charge for sex?"

The girl chuckled and rolled on the bed. She rose her head from the bed, looked at the man, and said, "Oh honey, I bet I could own this entire damn town if only I had a pussy to work with."

The Bad and the Terrible

Mark received a call from his lawyer, who insisted that they meet immediately. Mark arrived at the lawyer's office, and he was invited in. Once seated, the lawyer asked, "Should I give you the bad news first, or the terrible news?"

Mark is quiet for a moment before he says, "Well, if I have to choose between bad and terrible, I guess I could take the bad news first."

The lawyer says, "Your wife came across a picture worth half a million dollars."

"Is that the bad news?" Mark was stunned. "If that is bad, then I need to hear the terrible."

"The terrible news is that the picture was of your secretary and you."

You Started It

A fresh graduate of the Massachusetts Institute of Technology has gone for an interview for a job he applied for, and when he gets to the end of the interview, the interviewing Human Resource Officer asked, "And what amount are you expecting your salary to be?"

The young engineer replies, "About $125,000 per year, but that also depends on the benefits package you offer me."

The interviewer responds, saying, "Well, we could offer you 14 paid holidays, a five-week vacation, full dental and medical insurance, a company car leased every two years, perhaps a red Corvette, and a company retirement fund to 50 percent of your salary.

The young man is on the edge of his seat. He raises his arms in amazement and says, "Wow! Are you serious? Is that a joke?"

The HR officer replies, "I am only kidding, but you started it."

Not Giving You Any

In a local United Way office, the employees therein realize that they had never received any donation from the most successful lawyer in the town. The person responsible for calling out some new donors called him to persuade him to contribute. He said, "From the reports we have received, out of your $500,000 annual income, not even a single penny was given to charity. Wouldn't you be interested in giving back to the community, somehow?"

The successful lawyer was quiet for a moment before he replied, "I must ask, in your research, did you find out that I have a sickly mother who has been suffering from a long illness? Did it also reveal that her medical bills are a number of times bigger than her annual income?"

The United Way employee was more than embarrassed, and all he could mutter was, "Um, no..." The lawyer did not let him finish. He interrupted and said, "Or that I have a veteran disabled brother who, besides being confined to the wheelchair, is also blind?"

The troubled United Way representative tried to stammer out some apology, but the lawyer interrupted again. He said, "Or that my sister lost her husband in a traffic accident... Leaving her penniless to raise three children by herself?"

The United Way rep is now so humiliated, so beaten, and all he could say was, "I'm sorry, Sir. I did not know all that."

Again, the lawyer interrupted him and said, "Well, if I could not give my money to either of those people, how could I give it to you?"

Karma Is Bitchy

A business mogul flies to Las Vegas to have fun gambling for the weekend. At the casino, he loses everything, including the shirt off his back. At the end of the evening, he has nothing but a quarter in his pocket, and a return ticket back home. He figures that all he needs to do is find a way to get to the airport, and from there, he would be back home, free. He goes out to the front side of the casino and finds a cab waiting. He gets in and explains his situation to the cab driver, and promises that, on getting home, he would send the driver some money. For assurance, he offered the driver his driving license number, credit card numbers, and his address, amongst other details.

The cab driver would have none of it. He yelled, "If you haven't got the 15 dollars for this ride, get the hell out of my car!"

The businessman has no option but to hitchhike to the airport, and barely makes it in time to catch his flight.

A year goes by, and the businessman has accrued so much financial success. He returns to Vegas, and surprisingly, this time, he wins big. Feeling good and happy about himself, he goes to the front side of the casino to catch a cab ride to take him to the airport.

When he gets outside, who should he see at the end of the line of cabs but the old buddy that refused to give him a ride at the time when he was down on his luck!

The businessman stood and thought for a minute about how he would pay back the guy for his lack of compassion and empathy. He came up with a plan, and it sounded right.

The businessman approached the first cab in the line and asked, "How much to get to the airport?"

The first guy replied, "Fifteen bucks."

"How about if a blowjob on the way, how much would you charge me?"

"Shit! Get the heck away from my cab!"

The businessman went down the line of cabs, and with each of them, asked the same questions and got the same answer. At the end of the line, he got to his old friend, sat at the back seat, and asked, "How much to the airport?"

The man replied, "Fifteen bucks, Sir."

"Alright," the businessman replied.

The driver started the car ride to the airport, and as they slowly drove past the line of cabs, the businessman opened the window on his side and began to smile and give a thumbs up to the drivers in the cabs.

Big Guy

Guam, a man dressed in civilian clothing, was at the Andersen Air Force Base. He walked up to an airman and asked if he could be given a vehicle pass. The airman was fresh out of training, and he asked to see the driver's license, vehicle registration, and military ID. As the airman scrutinized the items handed to him, he noticed the abbreviations BG on the documents. He asked, "What do the letters BG stand for... Big Guy?"
The man replied as he leaned on the counter, "No, it's Brigadier General."

Drumming Up Business

A lawyer is just settling in a new town and has set up a new office in town. He started thinking of ways he could drum up business for his new office. While he is still thinking about it, a man enters the office, and on seeing him approaching, the lawyer sees that it is time to implement his little plan to impress the potential client.
The lawyer picks the phone lying on his desks and speaks as clearly as he can, "Well... Unfortunately, Sir, I am not in a position to take your case now because I am working on

some urgent cases full time. Kindly call me in one month so we can see whether I can help you."

The man is now at the lawyer's desk, and the attorney put down his phone. He asked the man waiting, "How may I help you, Sir?"

"I do not need legal help. I am an agent of the telephone communications company. I only came to make your phone connection."

The Heart Transplant

An elderly patient is in need of a heart transplant and is discussing his options with the doctor. The doctor tells him, "We have established three possible heart donors. One is a middle-aged businessman that has never smoked or drank, the second is of a healthy young athlete, and the third donor is of a lawyer who has just died after a 30-year career."

The patient replies, "I will have the lawyer's heart."

The doctor is taken back and asks, "Why do you prefer that heart?"

The patient answers, "That heart has never been used."

The Blonde at the Club

After work, two programmers are busy chatting sitting at the club. One of them says, "I bet you wouldn't believe me if I told you what I did yesterday. To start with, you need to know that I ran into a very beautiful blonde at the bar."

"So, what did you do?"

"I asked her to my place. We had some drinks, and after a while, the girl was begging me to undress her."

"Really? Are you serious? So, what happened next?"

"I pulled her dress and her blouse off of her and asked her to sit in my office, right next to the laptop I had just bought."

"Oh, really? You bought a new laptop? What model is it? What are its specifications?"

Get More Money

One day, the color of the printer color was looking a bit off, so the manager rang the local repair shop. The manager was surprised when the clerk announced that changing the color would cost about 50 dollars, and that if the manager found that too expensive, he might as well do the job himself. The manager was astonished, and he asked, "Does your boss know the manner in which you discourage business?"

"Sure," the clerk replied.

It had been the clerk's idea. Apparently, the business makes more money repairing the cleaning printers, and this often happens when the owners insist on doing the job themselves.

Leroy

An African American woman was at a welfare office filling some forms. One of the questions needed her to write the number of children she has. She wrote ten. In the section where she was required to list the names of her children, she only wrote 'Leroy.'

When the woman returned the forms, the lady behind the desk pointedout the mistake to the lady saying, "In the section that you are asked to list the names of your children, you were supposed to list the names of each of your ten children."

The black woman replied, "They are all called Leroy."

"Mmmh … that is quite unusual," the welfare worker responded, "So, when you call them, how do the kids know which of them you are talking to?"

"The black woman replied, "Oh, I call them by their last names."

Be More Tactful!

The Captain asked the Sergeant into his office and said to him, "Sarge, I just received a telegram saying that Private Jone's mother passed away yesterday. Go give him the news and send him over to see me." The Sergeant went over and called for his morning formation. When the troops had lined up, he began to scream his orders, "Listen up, soldiers! K.P. Smith, report to the Personnel for some signing, Johnson, report to the mess hall, and the rest of you report to the Motor Pool to do some maintenance work. Oh, I almost forgot, Jones, report to the Captain — your mother died." Later in the day, the Captain asked the Sergeant back in his office and rebuked him saying, "Sarge, that was one cold way to inform Private Jones that his mother had died. Next time, be a little more tactful!" The Sarge answered, "Yes, Sir."

A few months pass, and again, the Captain asked the Sergeant back into his office. He said, "Sarge, I just received a telegram saying that Private McGrath's mother has died. Go give him the news, and send him over to see me. This time, remember to be more tactful."

The Sergeant went and called for the morning formation. When the troops had lined up, he said, "Listen, men! Everyone who has a mother, take two steps forward!" He watched as the soldiers took steps forward. Catching a glimpse of Private McGrath doing the same, he shouted, "Not so fast, Private McGrath!"

First Come First Served

In a New York City restaurant, a waitress approaches one of the tables she is catering for the night and is shocked to find that the three Bulgarian businessmen seated at the table are furiously masturbating. She enquires, "What the heck are you guys doing?"

One of the men answered her, "You see, we are varrrree verrrry verrry hooongry."

The waitress motions a stroking move with her hand and asks them, "So, how will jerking off right here in the restaurant help to change that situation?"

The man replied, "On the menu is written, first come, first served!"

Voodoo Dick

A businessman was making arrangements ahead of his very long business trip he was to go on. One of the issues bothering his mind was that of his wife. He knew that she was the flirtatious kind, and he needed to get her something that would keep her occupied for the time he would be gone. He shook in fright at the thought of the possibility that someone might screw his wife while he was away.

The businessman got inside a sex toy shop and began to look around. He saw a life-sized sex doll, but thought it is not a good option because it too much resembled a real man. The man went to browse through the dildos displayed, looking for something that would truly please his wife. He approached the old man standing behind the counter, and explained his situation to him. The old man replied, "Well, I really do not know of anything that would successfully keep your wife occupied for the period you will be away. We got special attachments, vibrating dildos and so on... But I do not know of something that would keep her in check for weeks over, except..." The old man stopped.
The businessman was anxious to hear more, "Except what?"
"Nothing, Nothing."
"C'mon, I need something! Please tell me."

"Alright, Sir. I usually do not tell this to other customers, but there actually is a voodoo dick."

"Mmh... What's with this 'voodoo dick'?"

The old man bent over and reached for something from below the counter. He pulled out a wooden box on which strange symbols had been carved. He popped the box open, and there laid an ordinary-looking dildo.

The businessman looked at the contents of the box and let out a big laugh. He said, "Big deal! This thing looks like any other dildo you have in this shop."

The old man calmly replied, "But you are yet to see what it can do." The old man pointed his finger to the door and said, "Voodoo dick, to the door!"

The voodoo dick quickly shot out of the box and darted for the door. It began to screw the keyhole. The entire door started shaking from the large vibrations, and even a crack started to form right down the middle. Just when the door was about to split into two, the old man shouted, "Get back in your box, you voodoo dick!"

The voodoo dick stopped what it was doing immediately and floated across the room and back to the box. It simply lay there. Seeing this, the businessmanwas impressed. He shouted, "I'll take it."

The old man refused, and could not give in. He insisted that the dick was not for sale. However, when the businessman offered to pay $700 for it, the old man surrendered.

The man took his present to his wife and informed her that this was no ordinary dildo, and that if she needed to use it, all she had to do was give it an instruction saying, "Voodoo dick, into my pussy."

The man was satisfied that he had found the perfect solution for everything and that everything would be fine when he was away.

One day, when her husband had been gone for quite some days, the woman was unbearably horny. She wondered about several people she perceived would willingly satisfy her need, but her mind also drifted to the voodoo dick her husband had got her. She took it out and said the magic words, "Voodoo dick, my pussy!"

The magical dick shot right to her crotch and started thrusting. The experience was so good, nothing like anything she ever had.

After three mind-blowing orgasms, the woman thought that she had had enough and she made an attempt to pull the dick out. However, the dick remained adamant and would not get out. It continued to thrust. The lady made attempt after attempt to get it out with no results. Her husband had not told her how she would switch it off. The woman decided to go to the hospital to see if the doctors would help take it out.

She put on some clothes, got into the car, and started driving to the hospital. With every thrust, the woman would quiver.

As she drove to the hospital, she nearly veered off the road when she had another orgasm. A policeman driving behind her saw this and pulled her over. He demanded to see her license and registration and then asked whether she had been drinking. The woman was now twitching and gasping, but she managed to explain that she had not been drinking, and that she had a voodoo dick lodged in her pussy. She explained that however she tried, the dick would not stop screwing. The officer could not believe what she said and he said, "Oh sure! Voodoo dick, my ass!"

Check out other adult joke books:

Naughty Adult Joke Book: Dirty, Slutty, Funny Jokes That Broke The Censors – Jason S. Jones

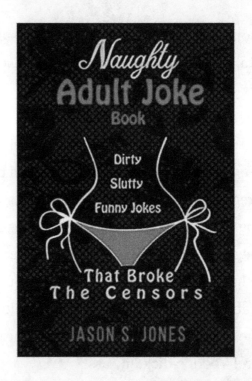

Why is a vagina similar to bad weather?

Once it wets, you have to go in.

CPSIA information can be obtained
at www.ICGtesting.com
Printed in the USA
BVHW031507261020
591816BV00004B/882